SEX
WAS
SEX

by

Marcena
&
Trevor Wyatt Moore

AVE MARIA PRESS & PILGRIM PRESS

176
m 78 s

7 / 46 7
October, 1970

SEX, SEX, SEX is a co-publishing project of Ave Maria Press, Notre Dame, Indiana, and Pilgrim Press, the trade imprint of United Church Press, Philadelphia, Pennsylvania.

Copyright 1969 Ave Maria Press, Notre Dame, Indiana 46556

Library of Congress Catalog Card Number: 69-18094

This book is dedicated to all tender,
loving cats; single, married,
or about to be;
under or over 30,
who are hip enough to want to dig
where their heads are at
as the so-called "sexual revolution"
rages 'round about them

and

to John Edward Williams,
friend, mentor, painter and graphic artist
extraordinaire
who, it is hoped, will not tear out his hair
in despair, nor abandon all hope
for a former disciple
when he sees what he's done
to Herr Gutenberg

TITLE

If you bought this book because of its you

won't be disappointed...

SEX!
SEX!
SEX!

because, Baby,
that's what
it's

ALL

ABOUT

1

but

IT COULD HAVE BEEN TITLED

LOVE

2

LOVE
LOVE
LOVE

because

4

LOVE

sex is a nothing

BUT HEY HEY HEY ₅

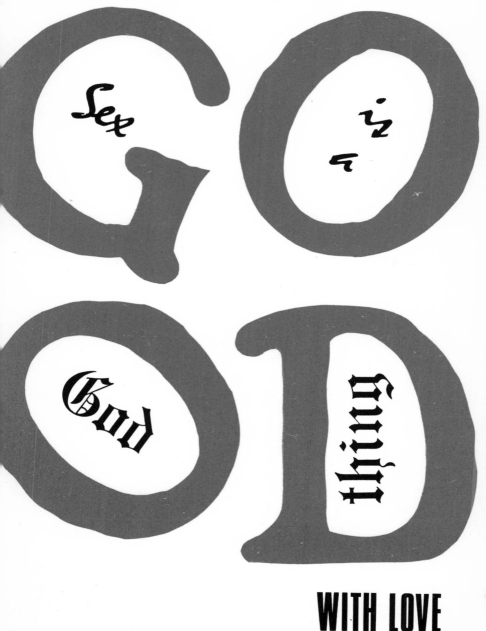

GIFT!

6

▶ more closely together in love ◀ ▶ ◀
▶ so that two persons may grow ◀

despite some other speculations to the contrary

multiplication of the species is not its sole purpose

SO IT'S

go

BUT

ter¹¹go

thereby

Friends

avoiding

Terrible Confusion

when called upon to

DISTINGUISH

FROM

LIGHT

If

YOU[17]

can't

dig

the

though you may

difference

have wallowed in wedlock

Baby

for 40 years

-18-

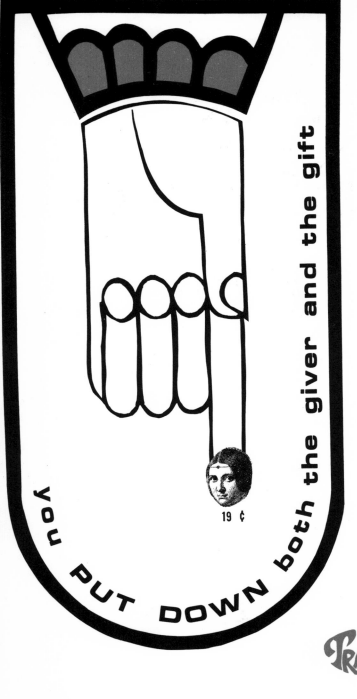

A real

PUT·ON too

small

WONDER

for there's been far

xxi

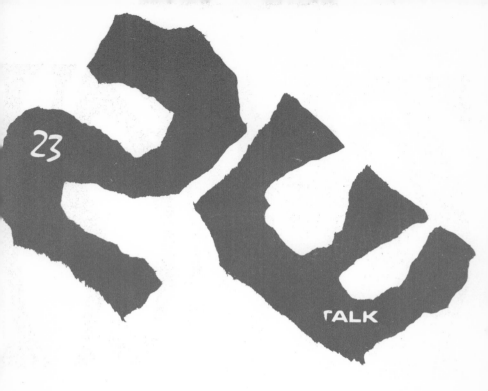

TALK
TALK

TALK
TALK
TALK

TALK
TALK
TALK
TALK

TALK
TALK

vingt-quatre

LOVE LOVE the

flexible **VERB** i you he

she it we they *just*

LOVE / LOVES

my your his her its their

that those

26

LIPSTICK	CAT
DOG	HAIRDO
CADILLAC	SWEATER
SKIRT	MOVIE
DISHWASHER	GRAND OLD FLA
SUIT	ROOM
LAWRENCE WELK	HAT
PERFUME	NECKLACE
WINE	SHOES
FLOWERS	SWIMMING POO
BOOK	DIAMONDS
AIR CONDITIONER	SHIRT
TV	RECORD
HOUSE	PAINTING
STEREO	PIZZA

ETC ETC

RE

these the

Things

Big & little

vegetable and mineral

27

ANIMATE and

IN

ANIMATE

of which 𝔖𝔱. 𝔓𝔞𝔲𝔩

was thinking

when he described LOVE as

something, Baby, with which

to
reckon?

??

HARDLY

like man it's

29

CONSTRUCTIVE

PATIENT

KIND

humble

Compassionate

ENDURING

GLAD

TRUTHFUL

UNSELFISH

freely given

HOPEFUL

believing

Trusting

EVERLASTING

FAITHFUL

forgiving

UNFAILING

XXX

the

True LOVE!

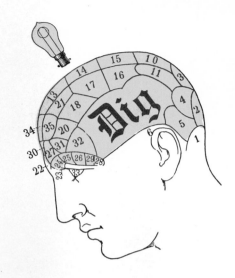

GROOVIEST

Made for people

YOU

JOY

even

it means **WORKING** at it

hard work
HUMAN work

**NOT
FOR
BIRDS
AND
BEES**

COMMITMENT

too

PRECIOUS

to

Lavish

on

34

36

not to put down

ROMANCE

Romance *is* GROOVY *too*

BUT

SHEER TIME

KIDS

HABIT

THE RAT RACE

PERPETUAL PROPINQUITY

OR

A HUNDRED OTHER THINGS

all

CONSPIRE

to
DAMPEN
BRING DOWN

ROMANCE

Shed but a wee tear, Lover

if you've dug LOVE

coming down from

the

ROMANTIC trip is

NO DRAG

like

R E A L I T Y

beats the

dream

40

it's the **REAL WORLD**

baby

WHERE THE

grooves ARE

WE

LEARN LOVE
MAKE LOVE

EMBRACE
SEX AS A
JOYOUS SIGN OF
ENDURING
COMMITMENT

41

COM

42

MIT

43

MEN

44

45

Like man, you mean

responsibility?

Well, Baby, that's, you know, where it's AT!

47

But
no need
to get

You know,
like
DIG,

commitment &
responsibility
make
like
RESPECT
man
&
without
THAT

you're

PLAYING
GAMES

&
USING
PEOPLE

like toys, man

and

LOVE

withers

&

DIES

52

WHILE

sex

becomes a

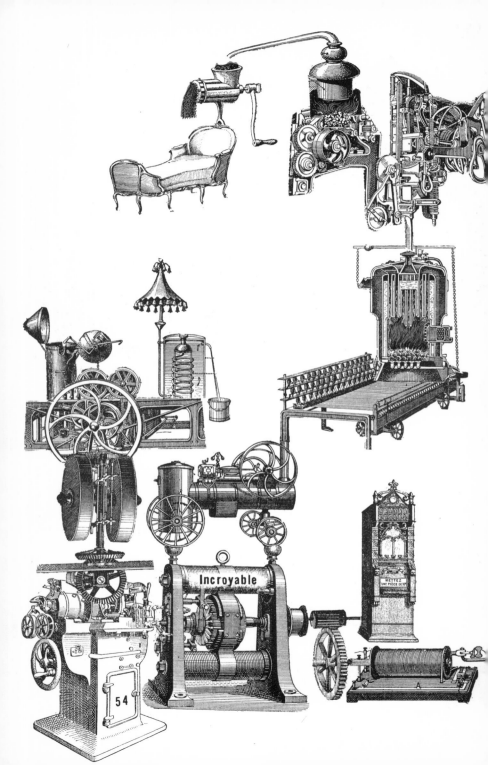

mere

PASSION

Machine

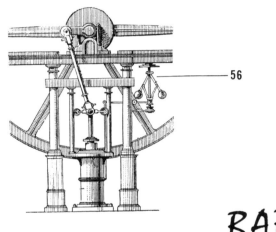

56

BABY

is

INCAPABLE

of

57

LIKE

DIG

BE

HUMAN

BABY

59

Assuming, *then, that*

COMMITMENT

☐ is   ☐ will soon be   ☐ has been for years
☐ I'm thinking about it, baby; don't come on so strong!
(Please check one.) FORM NO. XF-1984-a.

IS YOUR
BAG

There are
Some Things
about

SEX
&
LOVE

WHICH
EVERY
CAT
SHOULD
KNOW

BUT DIG
this book isn't a "how-to" manual

with charts; details

of

esoteric

preparations

exercises

positions

techniques

62

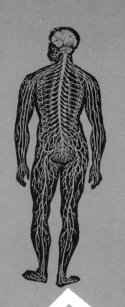

not

even

an

anatomy

lesson

nor
pious
prognostication
regarding
phases
of the moon
and family
planning

(or even the Pill) **63**

SORRY ABOUT THAT

NOT TO PUT DOWN ANY OF THAT jazz but over 100 BILLION

PRESENTING

EXPECTED to fumble

which LOVERS are

only A handful EVER go BEYOND

"MAZE of MECHANICAL"

BOOKS

on sex techniques ETC

through

TODAY & THE SCENE must be on

64

ACTION

while
INSTRUCTION
in these fascinating (wow) details is

great

& 𝕲𝕺𝕺𝕯

& NECESSARY

sometimes

we

get so

damned

HUNG UP

with

techniques

that *SEXUAL LOVE*

may become mere

to paraphrase the good Father Robert Capon

BED & BORED

most of the Great Lovers & Red Hot Chicks exist only
in Filmdom's Folklore anyway, baby

AT THE SAME TIME

confusing the MEDIUM with the MESSSAGE

come off it Marshall

there are always exceptions

67

which⁶⁸

isn't

where

it's

at

EVER

like

NOT ALL

SEXUAL LOVE

CONSISTS

OF

70

HORIZONTAL EXERCISES

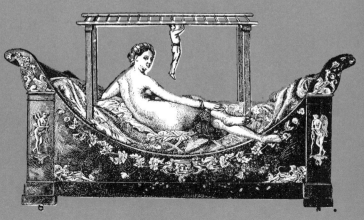

au contraire cheri

72

it's
freely
GIVING
one's self
to the other
rather than

perpetual

panting

pursuit

of

Internal
Combustion
that makes
LOVE

sexcessful

dig

the

cool cats

wow

LIKE

THEY

KNOW

THAT

75

sexual

com pat ibi lit y

so little of which appears to be around today

doesn't BEGIN with

MATTRESS

Mr. Hefner's PLAYBOY notwithstanding

EXPERTISE

to believe so
is as foolish as

like, you know, man
it's the other way

AROUND

Like dig
before the

PILLOW

comes the

PERSON

SPECIAL
creature
beloved by

GOD

78

person

some ONE

not someTHING

79

beloved by GOD

can you do less?

person

THE

**COOL
CATS**
are
PERSONS usually
hip enough to
forego sex until
they have
COMMITTED
themselves
to
Each Other

a lot of rap about COMMITMENT?

IT MAY BE AN OLD FASHIONED WORD

but so is Sex and

*without committed love
the whole scene gets
distorted as hell*

like baby, no matter how high the fever may rise,

when it breaks, two uncommitted persons

may find themselves just used,

lonely people, utter

strangers

like

nowhere

COMMITMENT *means* LOVE *that wills intensely the greatest good of the one loved*

82

$\mathcal{E}$

Marriage

r.s.v.p.   *83*

*(after more or less
relevant
& costly ceremonies)* *****

is generally regarded
as the state of life
most suitable
for fulfillment
of mutual commitments

84

for chicks and their mommas who believe that a big church wedding
is the end (or even the beginning) of the story

we have built for them here a **damned big church**

＊N.B.: "ceremonies'

whether you are to be / hope to be / were

Wed

at

or

THE LITTLE BROWN CHURCH IN THE VALE

86

before

the

or

The Rev. Mr. John Smith

87

were / will be / are

the <u>actual</u>

Ministers

of **YOUR** union

a clergyman, acting for the People of God,
witnesses your vows,
calls down the blessings of the Holy Spirit upon them,
but he doesn't "marry" you.

YOU marry EACH OTHER!

minister (min′is-tẽr)**, n. 1.** one who serves. **v.t. 1.** to supply; provide. **v.i. 1.** to give help; fill needs.

ministry (min′is-tri)**, n. 1.** the act of ministering, serving.

each other, that is.

..nd baby, while this ministry may begin with "I will",

it doesn't
end
in a foolish fusillade
of rice at the
church door

but continues
to work, to grow,
to fulfill, to serve;
to share
bodies, minds, hopes,
dreams, goals, bitter
disappointments & often
dull demands of daily
living

man!

this "ministry" bit

raises hell with

Squaresville

interpretations of

St. Paul's

paradox: while he could describe lov
eloquently enough, man! did he ever put down wome
and slaves - and sex - like wow

notion that the

You

Know

Who

is

it

... in bed

in the home

in the world

(& in the Church)

BUT

a mutual ministry of love

which shares weakness as well as strength

**can't buy such
a supposition
without
reservation**

&

94

**must also invent
some new math
to reinterpret**

**the OLD EQUATION
which states:**

$$1 + 1 = 1$$

OR

TWO

BECOME

ONE

which they do
– but without the

SUPER
IMPO
SITION

of

**character
& personality**

USUALLY ASSOCIATED
WITH THE 2 - in - 1 BIT

this'll never work, because they're

individual

s

INDIVIDUAL

&

each

has

gotta

do

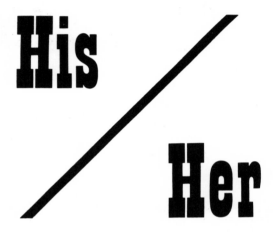

99

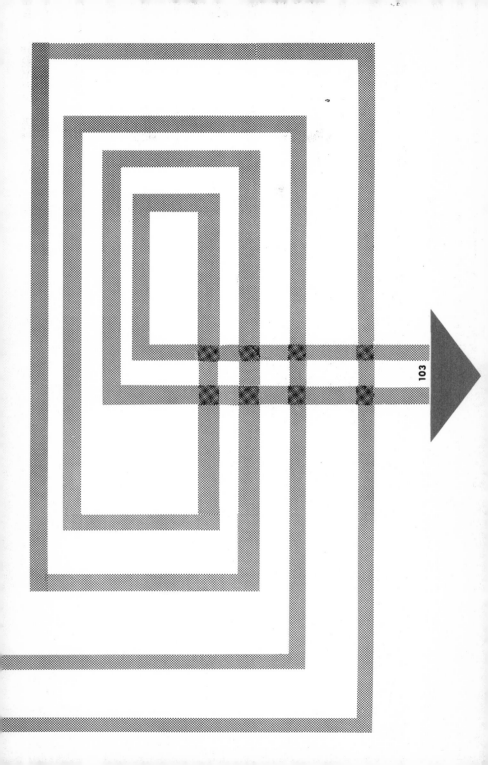

103

and each

respect

the

other's

thing

making the two-in-one relationship something like this ▶

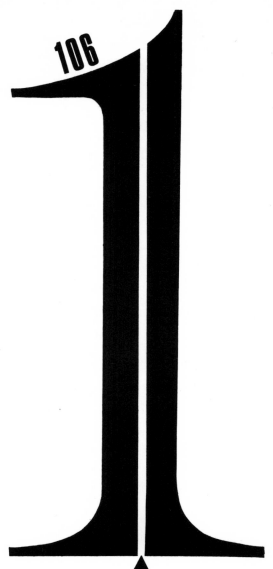

106

with an a p a r t n e s s amidst the
oneness
that permits individual personalities
(and respect for them)
to develop & flourish

but dig . . .

even with this necessary

slight

apart

ness

EACH

is

inc_mpl_te

without

the

OTHER

like

baby
EACH
NEEDS
the
OTHER
intellectually / psychically / physically
spiritually / sexually

happily, these continual demands never

DRAIN

the wellsprings of love which, like a recirculating fountain, replenish themselves with each

FUL**FILL**MENT

of one another's needs

& dig this, too, baby

while this whole boss bag begins, usually,

with mutually irresistible physical
pow! *attraction*

the greatest sexual
FULFILLMENT
(not KICKS, baby; that's a different scene)

comes from

HEAD
SHARING

because that's where it's AT

110

like 'soul'
like knowing
ONE ANOTHER

an unfolding REVELATION

which removes hang ups
& reservations

which may

inhibit love's

sexual response to love

& like, you can't put down
the 'flesh' nor should you;

like man! it's HERE

& we live in our skins

FURTHER, the flesh

is so
GOOD
that
GOD
Himself
put it on
and even promised to
Resurrect
it
like
WOW!
HUMAN!
Glory
MINE!
Hallelujah!
YOURS!

112

NO OTHER ANIMAL CAN MAKE THIS CLAIM!

good news

if awesome

& if you dig the message, you'll begin to dig each other & realize that sex is truly a

Holy

sanctified

human

act

115

the Liturgy
of your committed
Ministry of Love

it's **YOUR** Thing

Only **YOU** can do it

& Nobody, but **NO ONE**
else can make decisions
for **YOU** about how
to do it

BECAUSE YOU LOVE

BECAUSE YOU'RE HUMAN

RESPONSIBLE

REDEEMED

because, baby,
YOU'RE

THE BEGINNING

120